LIFE IS BEAUTIFUL

Laura Shenton

LIFE IS BEAUTIFUL

Laura Shenton

Iridescent Toad Publishing

Iridescent Toad Publishing.

©Laura Shenton 2023
All rights reserved.

Laura Shenton asserts the moral right to be identified as the author of this work.

No part of this publication may be reproduced, stored or transmitted in any form or by any means, electronic, mechanical, photocopying, recording, scanning, or otherwise without written permission from the publisher. It is illegal to copy this book, post it to a website, or distribute it by any other means without permission.

Cover art by Obsessed by Books Designs

First edition. ISBN: 978-1-913779-27-6

*There's a lot of beauty in life.
Even in dark times where it may be harder to see it.*

The purpose of this book is to embrace the joys of what's there.

Through positive poetry...

Life
Hatching out from the cocoon of an egg

Welcome to the world
Sweet baby bird

The glory of the warm orange light
Bursting through the window
To welcome you
To the joys of a new day

Friendship is powerful

Not merely people
To do stuff with

Someone who "gets" you
Your humour
And your weird little quirks

Someone you could hug
And snuggle
Under a duvet of emotion
And loyalty
Forever

Good times are evident
In how they feel
Comparatively better
Than bad times

Feel that difference
Enjoy the moment

No matter how crazy it gets
No matter how wild the world
Flowers
Never stop growing

An infinite number of colours
Make a technicolour world

It's just as bright and bold
As it is dull and dark

Life's too short
To try all the food
To hear all the music
To meet all the people
To experience it all

The cake won't be there forever
So take a big tasty bite, and enjoy

Sometimes we all
Need a little help
And have a little vice
And that's ok

Show me the way
To the most magical place
You can think of

I want to know you
I want to breathe with you

Crispy crunchy leaves
Beneath the feet
That walk the path
Through a new autumn

Winter brings spring
And from there, summer
Seasons are too short
To dread the weather

Blue sky
Red sky
Grey sky

It's all a fascinating blanket

Every face in the crowd
Has a story to tell

There is always love
Even when people
Might struggle to show it

Of course there is evil
Not everyone
Has emotional intelligence
But maybe that's just humans
Being humans

And there's still always love
Even through the flaws
There's always some kind of love

To gaze into your eyes
And get lost in them

And in the very essence
Of who you are

Wow

The scent of a roundabout
Adorned with flowers

Even in traffic
The sensory thrives

Teeth
Are incredible
Chomp chomp chomp

Show me your smile

My dog was awesome
So cuddly, so friendly
That sweet calming smell
Of warm biscuits
And baby powder

He's not here anymore
But he had a good life

The smell of a freshly-cooked breakfast
To start the day
All the textures and flavours
One plate can display

Do what truly nourishes you

Every. Single. Day.

The buzz of the bees
Working hard by the trees
Flying home in the breeze
Through the nest they do squeeze

You don't have to be Snow White
To be in harmony with the birdsong

Stood in the shower
Feeling the comforting jet
Of strong warm water
Punctuated with the smell
Of lilies, apples or lemons
Whatever your choice
Of shower gel

Taking a hot bubble bath
A calming evening
With the window open
To a soft pink sky

No matter who you are
And where you're heading
Someone, somewhere
Will hold your hand

Maybe you know who
Maybe you don't
But they're definitely out there
Caring for you

The song of a thousand angels
Or a dog barking in the night

The glow of the moon
Throws light on it all

Every day
The sun rises
And then it sets
No matter what

A good day
Or a bad day
The world
Keeps going

In the peak of the summer
Conkers start to form
Green spiky shells
Protecting their fruit

Along comes the autumn
The green shells break open
Nature punctuates
The passing of time

Waking up
To a new day
You're not in a rush
Your sleepy head is cocooned
By the softest pillow
And your whole body is safe
Under the warmest blanket

A hut in the forest
It doesn't matter if it rains
It doesn't matter if it snows
The hut provides shelter
No matter what

It's nice to be inside the hut
But when outside of it
There's always that hope
That soon
You'll be inside

The warm glow of the room
Emphasised by a loyal pet
Curled up asleep
Next to you on the sofa

Paint a picture
And watch the paint flow

An exciting new world
Into which your mind goes

So much life
Deep down in the ocean
What's on the land
Is just the tip of the iceberg

On and on it goes
Down into an eternity
Of a whole new world
Beyond just what we know

Warm winter food
And a lovely hot drink
All your friends with you
If not in body, then in spirit

There are certainly people in this life
Who are kind and helpful
Without extra motive

The goodness of the human heart
Not always publicised
But certainly true

Baking in the oven
Sit the fresh cakes
Lovingly made
By someone who cares

The smallest flame
Can illuminate
Even the darkest room

With the lines penned on his hand
In blue biro
The actor gave a stellar performance

No lies, no deceit
His methods hurt no one
Whatever it takes
To get the job done
And get it done well
Don't sweat it

When the gravity
Of a situation
Feels weighted
Heavy
And deeply-rooted
There will come a time
Where it is less so

In a room that feels stale
Overbearing and foreboding
Look at a painting on the wall
Or out through the window

There is always, always
An escape route
Where needed

Close your eyes
Just for this moment

You are floating on water

It can take your weight
Peaceful and calm
In the stillness

Curled up in bed
With your eyes closed
Someone who loves you
Is holding you

If not in person
Then in their mind

A day so pretty
With weather so gorgeous
That several butterflies
Can be seen
All at once

Dancing in the sun
A beautiful kaleidoscope
Making shapes
On the fragrance
Of the breeze

As winter draws near
With the lights on indoors
Outside is a squirrel
Preparing to nest

Collecting and planning
For warmth in his den
With plenty of food
'Til he comes out again

A big fluffy towel
After a nice long shower

White hot lightning
Cracking through the sky
Breaking the muggy mist
Cleansing the day

Options and freewill
Can be powerful combinations

Don't be afraid to think

You just never know
Who you'll meet today

They could change your life
In a wonderful way

Sunflowers

Brief in their prime
But still in their time
They grow big and bold

Everyone can grow cress
With minimal knowledge
Of gardening

Plant those seeds
And watch them sprout
Into something delicious

A beautiful day for a walk
A beautiful day for a drive
A beautiful day for an open window
Whether you're indoors or out

Don't think too much

Thinking too much
Is an easy trap
To get caught in

You don't need to have
All of the answers

You're just one person
And that's ok

When a friendly cat
Sits on your lap
Because like a kindred spirit
They know you need comfort

You're allowed
To make mistakes

Anyone who says otherwise
Mustn't be listened to

Mistakes are part of
The learning curve
On the path
To greater things

When you radiate
Positive energy
It can attract and inspire
Others who need it

You're alive today
Embrace the opportunity
As you feel the power
Of each breath

Even when life feels
Like it's too much
In through the nose
And out through the mouth

You're here
In the present
And there's still everything
To play for

The soul knows
How to love
Like the heart knows
How to beat

Don't underestimate
The wisdom
Of your experience

You've got this

Create something

Because you can

Peppers are so shiny
So much impact
From a crisp juicy bite

Every petal
On every flower
Makes the garden
What it is

With a little help, and a little love
Wounds can heal

Another person's beauty
Doesn't rob you of your own

Everyone rocks
Everyone glows

It's cold out there
I'll put the kettle on
Let's have a brew
And a damn good chat

The joys of an early night
There's still lots to do
But it will be done much better
After a good night's sleep

Humans are super adaptable
It's in our genes

When hit
With the shock of change
There are things we can do
To get back up
And running

The needle
Goes onto the record
And follows the spiral
Through in a journey

Maybe the weatherman's right
Maybe the weatherman's wrong

It doesn't matter

What one person finds beautiful
Might be very different
To what another person
Finds beautiful

And that, in and of itself
Is, errr…

Beautiful!

A sleepy puppy
Tired from a long day
Of fun
And exploring

When his batteries are recharged
What will his next adventure bring?

It's always good
To feed the birds

A small effort
Makes a big difference

To both

The winged ones get fed
While the humans enjoy the view

You can never have
Too many photos
Of your beloved pet

All creatures great and small

It's powerful to be stoic
With a poker face

It's powerful to cry
And let it all out

Absolutely no shame
In either of those

Dolphins

So intelligent
So emotional
So caring
So brave
So bold

As the wolf howls at the moon
A rhythm and melody
Beyond human comprehension
Echoes across a blanket of sky

Every spot on a Dalmatian
Dit-di-dit-dit-dot

Cuddly snuggly
Cookies and cream

It's been a long day
But that's ok
You're home now

Winter solstice
Brings a promise
Of longer days, brighter days

Summer solstice
Brings the comfort
Of nights in, time to reflect

Your voice matters
Don't hide
Don't shout
Just be

Seeing a true friend
Isn't a chore

If their company is fulfilling
Then naturally
You'll be back for more

Curious cows
Coming closer to the fence
That separates them
From the humans

The beautiful bovines
Just want to say hello
In between grazing
On the lush green grass

The gentle flow of the river
Accompanying the sounds
Of your footsteps
As you walk along the path nearby

The distinctive smell of home
Consciously or subconsciously
It always strikes a chord

Talk to me
I'm listening

The waves
Eternally moving

The tide
Reliably changing

The comfort
Of the never-ending

Every star in the sky
Shining brightly

Stunning flecks
Of cosmic glitter
Against the navy
Cloak of night

Our time on the earth
Isn't forever

Use it wisely

Dear world
You are big and round
And there's a lot going on
But no matter what happens
You are our home

From the sparkling skies
To the dusky depths
Of the infinite ocean
There is so much beauty
For the eye to see

In the course of one lifetime
We won't see it all
But the fact that it's there
Calling, imploring, inviting
You to engage

That alone
Is worth all the fish in the sea
All the stars in the sky
All the grass in the field
All the flowers in the garden

Breathe

www.ingramcontent.com/pod-product-compliance
Lightning Source LLC
Chambersburg PA
CBHW041147110526
44590CB00027B/4160